Sylvan Park

Sitting Bull

1831–1890

by Anne M. Todd

Content Consultant:
Robert L. Munkres, Professor Emeritus
Author and Lecturer
Muskingum College
New Concord, Ohio

Blue Earth Books

an imprint of Capstone Press
Mankato, Minnesota

Blue Earth Books are published by Capstone Press
151 Good Counsel Drive, P.O. Box 669, Mankato, Minnesota 56002
http://www.capstone-press.com

Copyright ©2003 by Capstone Press. All rights reserved.
No part of this publication may be reproduced in whole or in part,
or stored in a retrieval system, or transmitted in any form or by any means,
electronic, mechanical, photocopying, recording, or otherwise,
without written permission of the publisher.
For information regarding permission,
write to Capstone Press, 151 Good Counsel Drive,
P.O. Box 669, Dept. R, Mankato, Minnesota 56002
Printed in the United States of America.

Library of Congress Cataloging-in-Publication Data
Todd, Anne, M.
    Sitting Bull, 1831–1890 / by Anne M. Todd.
        p. cm. — (American Indian biographies)
    Summary: Explores the life of the Lakota leader, Sitting Bull, including the battles in which he fought, his surrender and death. Includes activities, sidebars, a map, and a chronology.
    Includes bibliographical references and index.
    ISBN 0-7368-1215-6 (hardcover)
    1. Sitting Bull, 1834?–1890—Juvenile literature. 2. Dakota Indians—Biography—Juvenile literature. 3. Dakota Indians—History—Juvenile literature. 4. Hunkpapa Indians—Biography—Juvenile literature. [1. Sitting Bull, 1834?–1890. 2. Dakota Indians—Biography. 3. Dakota Indians—History. 4. Hunkpapa Indians—Biography. 5. Indians of North America—Great Plains—Biography. 6. Kings, queens, rulers, etc.] I. Title. II. Series.
E99.D1 S6235 2003
978.004'9752—dc21   2001008224

Editorial Credits
Editor: Katy Kudela
Cover Designer: Heather Kindseth
Interior Layout Designers: Jennifer Schonborn and
    Heather Kindseth
Interior Illustrator: Jennifer Schonborn
Production Designers: Jennifer Schonborn and
    Gene Bentdahl
Photo Researcher: Mary Englar

Photo Credits
Denver Public Library, cover, 4, 21, 25, 27 (bottom), 29 (top right); Colorado Historical Society, cover (war whistle), 13, 18; Art Resource, 7; Joseph E. Velazquez, 5; Hulton/Archive by Getty Images, 8, 16, 17, 22, 23, 27 (top); Philbrook Museum, Tulsa, Oscar Howe (1951.8), 9, Oscar Howe (1949.29.9), 20; Sid Richardson Collection, 10; Fort St. Joseph Museum, 11, 29 (top left); Jeroen Vogtschmidt, 12, 29 (bottom); National American Archives (negative 3195-g), 14; Capstone Press/Gary Sundermeyer, 15; University of Nebraska Press, 19; Minnesota Historical Society, 24; "Hope Springs Eternal," Howard Terpning, Greenwich Workshop, 26; Woolaroc Museum, 28

1 2 3 4 5 6 07 06 05 04 03 02

Contents

Chapter 1
Lakota Battle for Homeland   4

Chapter 2
A Lakota Boy   8

Chapter 3
Leader for His People   12

Chapter 4
Struggles with White People   16

Chapter 5
Lakota Fight for Their Land   20

Chapter 6
Lakota Life Changes   24

Features

    Map   6

    Chronology   29

    Words to Know   30

    To Learn More   31

    Internet Sites   31

    Places to Visit   31

    Index   32

CHAPTER 1
Lakota Battle for Homeland

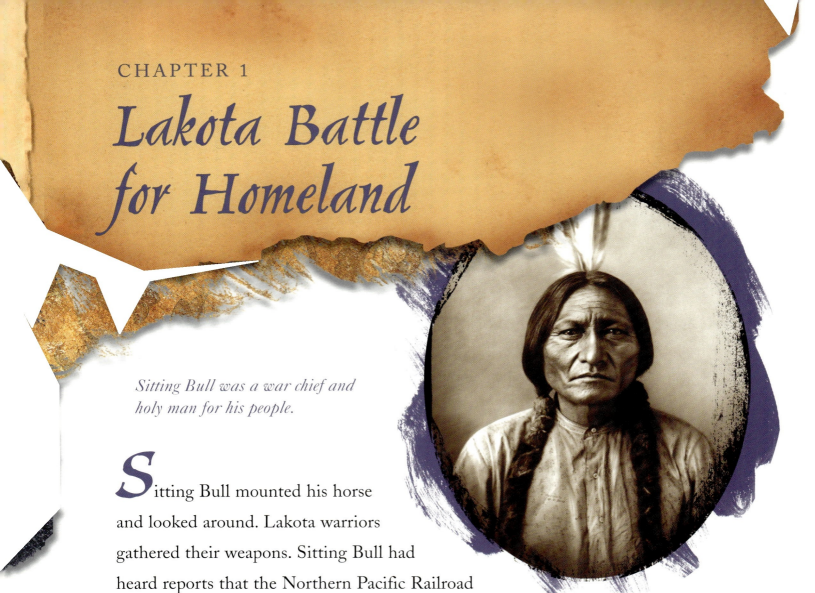

Sitting Bull was a war chief and holy man for his people.

Sitting Bull mounted his horse and looked around. Lakota warriors gathered their weapons. Sitting Bull had heard reports that the Northern Pacific Railroad company was planning a route directly through Lakota land.

Sitting Bull wanted peace for his people. If the white people built a railroad, they would also build towns around the railroad. These plans threatened the Lakota way of life. Sitting Bull would do what was necessary to protect his people's land.

Sitting Bull and a band of Lakota warriors rode to the soldiers' camp. As the warriors neared the camp, the soldiers began shooting. Sitting Bull and the Lakota warriors were face-to-face with 500 U.S. soldiers who had been sent to protect the Northern Pacific Railroad's land surveyors.

Lakota warriors fought many battles to protect their land.

The year was 1872. The Battle of Arrow Creek began before daybreak. As the sun began to rise, many Lakota were wounded and several had died.

Sitting Bull would not allow the soldiers to kill all his warriors. He needed to get the warriors' attention and end the battle. This feat would prove his leadership. Sitting Bull laid down his gun and walked onto the battlefield. He calmly looked at the lines of U.S. soldiers on one side and American Indian warriors on the other. Sitting Bull pulled his pipe out of its bag and pushed a pinch of tobacco into the pipe's bowl.

He then called for the other Lakota warriors to prove their bravery by sitting with him on the battlefield.

Four Lakota warriors came forward. Sitting Bull could see they were anxious to get back to the Lakota line. Soldiers and other warriors continued to battle around them. Bullets whizzed past. Sitting Bull invited his fellow warriors to sit down. He lit the pipe, puffed the smoke, and passed it around to the other warriors.

As each of these warriors took a turn smoking the pipe, Sitting Bull prayed to Wakantanka, the Great Spirit, for courage to end the battle.

After the warriors finished smoking the pipe, Sitting Bull cleaned it out and placed it back in his pipe pouch. As he slowly walked off the battlefield, Sitting Bull watched the four warriors run back to the Lakota line. When Sitting Bull returned to the Lakota line, he shouted, "That's enough. We must quit."

The Battle of Arrow Creek ended without a winner. Sitting Bull and his warriors had proven they would not watch peacefully while the U.S. soldiers interfered with Lakota land.

Today, Sitting Bull is remembered as a brave leader who fought for the rights of the Lakota people.

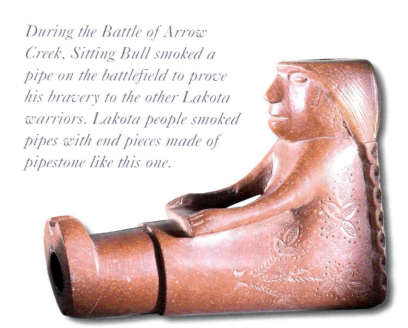

During the Battle of Arrow Creek, Sitting Bull smoked a pipe on the battlefield to prove his bravery to the other Lakota warriors. Lakota people smoked pipes with end pieces made of pipestone like this one.

CHAPTER 2
A Lakota Boy

Northern Plains Indians, such as the Lakota, relied on the buffalo for their food and clothing.

Sitting Bull was born about 1831 into the Hunkpapa band of the Lakota. The Hunkpapa is one of seven bands that make up the Lakota tribe. The Lakota were nomadic, moving their camp from place to place following the buffalo herds.

The Hunkpapa band camped in the grassy plains west of the Missouri River in present-day North Dakota, South Dakota, and Montana. They also occupied areas south of the Yellowstone River in present-day Montana and Wyoming.

As a young boy, Sitting Bull spent his days playing games and listening to the elders of his tribe.

Sitting Bull was born in the village of Many-Caches. This village was located on the south side of the Grand River in present-day South Dakota.

Sitting Bull's parents named him Jumping Badger, but no one called him by that name. Instead, people called him Hunk-es-ni, which means Slow. He made careful moves when he walked or played, and the name described his actions.

Slow's father was named Tatanka-Iyotanka, which means Sitting Bull. He was a Lakota leader. Slow's mother was called Her-Holy-Door. She was known as a happy woman who liked to tell stories.

At the time of Slow's birth, Sitting Bull and Her-Holy-Door had two daughters. Good Feather was older than Slow, and Brown-Shawl Woman was younger.

As a boy, Slow had dreams of becoming a great hunter and warrior. He practiced his skills with a bow and arrows. Slow hunted small game, such as rabbits and birds.

When he was 10 years old, Slow killed his first buffalo. He quickly became a successful hunter. He often gave his kill to the elders and widows in his village. Slow's people greatly valued his generosity.

Northern Plains Indian warriors often counted coup during battle.

At age 14, Slow won his first war honor by counting coup. During this brave act, a warrior touched the enemy with his hand or coup stick and escaped unharmed. Slow got his chance to count coup when he followed a group of older Lakota warriors on a horse-raiding party. During the fight, Slow touched a Crow warrior with his coup stick. "I, Slow, have conquered him!" he shouted.

Returning home, Slow's family prepared a celebration in his honor. During the feast, Slow received a single white eagle feather from his father. To recognize his son's courage, Sitting Bull performed a name changing ceremony for Slow. Sitting Bull called to his son, "I give you my name. From this day forward you will be called Tatanka-Iyotanka." Sitting Bull's father then took the name Jumping Bull.

Drawing Pictographs

Sitting Bull enjoyed telling stories to his family and friends. Along with telling stories, he made drawings called pictographs. Sitting Bull used these pictographs to record important events in his life. You can make your own pictograph and share it with your family and friends.

What You Need

paper

pencil

colored pencils or crayons

What You Do

1. Think about an important event in your life or a time when you were proud of yourself.
2. With a pencil, draw this event on a piece of paper.
3. Add color to the drawing with colored pencils or crayons.
4. Share your pictograph with your family and friends. Ask if they can understand the pictograph's story.

Counting coup was an important event in Sitting Bull's life. He recorded his coup with pictographs. This pictograph was drawn by Sitting Bull.

CHAPTER 3

Leader for His People

This painting shows an older Sitting Bull wearing the clothing of the Strong Hearts. Sitting Bull became a Strong Heart at age 21.

At the age of 20, Sitting Bull married a Lakota woman named Light Hair. Sitting Bull was known as a kind-hearted man who loved children. He was happy to start his own family.

When Sitting Bull was 21 years old, he became a member of the Strong Hearts. This group of warriors showed their bravery and battle skills during wars against enemy tribes. Few warriors earned the honor of becoming a Strong Heart.

Northern Plains Indians used shields in battles and spiritual ceremonies.

In 1856, Sitting Bull and a group of warriors went on a horse-raiding party to an enemy Crow camp. They quietly rounded up the horses and began their trip home. As the sun began to rise, a group of Crow appeared in the distance. The Crow caught up to the Lakota group. They fought to recapture their horses.

During the battle, Sitting Bull fought a Crow warrior dressed in a red shirt trimmed with white fur. This clothing was reserved for a chief.

Sitting Bull shot the Crow chief. As the chief was dying, he fired his gun. The bullet hit Sitting Bull in the foot. This wound caused Sitting Bull to walk with a limp for the rest of his life.

Sitting Bull earned a great honor by killing an enemy chief. He was named a member of the Midnight Strong Heart Society. Only the finest Strong Hearts were allowed into this Lakota society.

During this same year, Sitting Bull also became a holy man, called a Wichasha Wakan. As a holy man, he often spoke to Wakantanka, the Great Spirit. Sitting Bull's dreams gave him visions of future events.

In 1857, Sitting Bull became a war chief of the Hunkpapa band. He was grateful to be given this honor. He would later receive yet another great honor. Sitting Bull was named the head chief of the Lakota nation. This event occurred sometime during the late 1860s.

In 1857, Light Hair died while giving birth to a son. Sitting Bull's son later died of disease at age 4. Sitting Bull was troubled by the death of his son. He felt it was important to pass on his knowledge. He adopted his nephew, One Bull. Sitting Bull enjoyed teaching him the skills of a warrior.

Around this time, Sitting Bull also adopted a young boy from another tribe as his brother. He gave his adopted brother the name Stays Back.

Sitting Bull missed his wife and son. He took two wives, Red Woman and Snow-on-Her. In Lakota culture, men sometimes had several wives.

Sitting Bull had two daughters with Snow-on-Her. He also had a son with Red Woman.

Sitting Bull enjoyed time spent with his family. But Sitting Bull's wives did not get along. Sitting Bull finally told Snow-on-Her to leave. In 1871, Red Woman died. Sitting Bull was left alone with three children.

In 1872, Sitting Bull married Four Robes. He also married her sister, Seen-by-the-Nation. The two sisters remained with Sitting Bull until his death.

Sitting Bull is pictured here with his daughter, grandson, and mother, Her-Holy-Door.

Plum Muffins

Sitting Bull and his family likely ate many dishes prepared with fruits. As a nomadic tribe, the Lakota gathered fruit and vegetables. They rarely grew crops.

What You Need

Ingredients

1 cup (250 mL) dried cherries*
1 cup (250 mL) boiling water
1 16-ounce (480-gram) can of
    purple plums, drained and pitted
½ cup (125 mL) vegetable oil
4 cups (1,000 mL) flour
1½ teaspoons (7 mL) salt
1½ teaspoons (7 mL) allspice
1 teaspoon (5 mL) ground cloves
1 cup (250 mL) honey
½ cup (125 mL) pure maple syrup
    *may substitute dried cranberries

Equipment

small glass bowl
liquid measuring cup
muffin pans
non-stick cooking spray
large mixing bowl
potato masher or fork
wooden mixing spoon
dry-ingredient measuring cups
measuring spoons
large spoon
wire cooling rack

What You Do

1. Preheat oven to 350°F (180°C).
2. Place dried cherries in small glass bowl and cover with boiling water. Let stand 30 minutes until dried fruit begins to plump.
3. Apply non-stick cooking spray to inside of muffin pans. Set aside.
4. With potato masher or fork, mash plums in a large mixing bowl. Add remaining ingredients and mix well.
5. Add soaked cherries and the liquid to muffin batter, blending well.
6. Use a large spoon to scoop batter into the muffin pans. Fill each muffin cup half full with batter.
7. Bake muffins 25 to 30 minutes.
8. Remove the muffin pans from the oven. Cool pans on a wire rack for 10 minutes. Turn muffin pan upside down to remove muffins.

Makes about 2 dozen muffins

CHAPTER 4
Struggles with White People

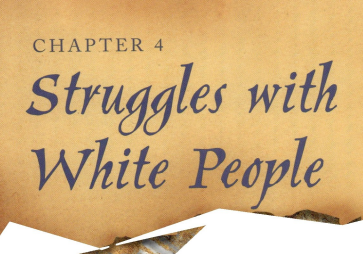

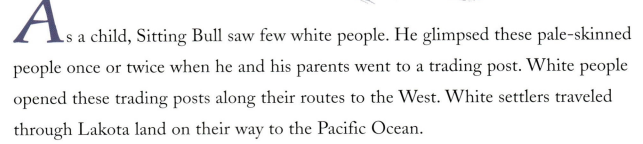

Many settlers traveled to the western United States to start a new life.

As a child, Sitting Bull saw few white people. He glimpsed these pale-skinned people once or twice when he and his parents went to a trading post. White people opened these trading posts along their routes to the West. White settlers traveled through Lakota land on their way to the Pacific Ocean.

In 1843, white settlers began following the Oregon Trail. This pathway began in a place the settlers called Independence, Missouri. From this point, settlers traveled about 2,000 miles (3,200 kilometers) to the Pacific Northwest in present-day Washington and Oregon. These routes were south of the Hunkpapa camp.

In 1851, the U.S. government proposed the Fort Laramie Treaty. The government wanted to build roads and military posts on American Indian land. In exchange for the land, the U.S. government promised supplies and protection from white trespassers. The treaty also created territorial boundaries.

By 1863, Sitting Bull and his people could no longer avoid the soldier chiefs. General Alfred Sully and his troops were sent to North Dakota to capture the Dakota Indians who fled from Minnesota during the Dakota Conflict of 1862.

Sitting Bull fought his first battle against the U.S. soldiers in 1864. Even though Sitting Bull and his warriors fought bravely, more than 100 warriors died in this battle.

In 1866, white settlers began traveling across Lakota land from

Fort Laramie was located in present-day Wyoming. The Lakota came here to trade and receive the food and supplies promised under the Fort Laramie Treaty.

Wyoming to Montana. They were searching for gold. The settlers called this route the Bozeman Trail.

In August 1866, Sitting Bull heard reports that soldiers were building Fort Buford at the junction of the Yellowstone and Missouri rivers. As war chief, Sitting Bull promised to defend his land. Sitting Bull and his warriors led raids against the soldiers at this fort.

At the same time, other Lakota attacked three forts located along the Bozeman Trail. On December 21, 1866, Red Cloud, a Lakota chief, led an attack near Fort Phil Kearny, Wyoming. Red Cloud and his warriors defeated Captain William Fetterman and his entire command.

The U.S. government was stunned by the Fetterman fight and the attacks that followed. Government officials held a peace council at Fort Laramie.

The Fort Laramie Treaty of 1868 created the Great Sioux Reservation. The treaty gave the Lakota all the land

Many Northern Plains Indians carried their pipes in decorated pipe bags.

in present-day South Dakota west of the Missouri River.

The Lakota chiefs who signed the treaty did not understand that their people would be placed on reservations. Sitting Bull did not believe these promises, so he did not sign the treaty.

In 1874, Lieutenant Colonel George Custer came to South Dakota with 1,000 men to explore the Black Hills. Gold was found during the exploration. Custer sent a scout to Fort Laramie to telegraph the news.

Sitting Bull and Crazy Horse gathered Lakota and Cheyenne warriors together in preparation for the Battle of the Little Bighorn. About 3,000 American Indians gathered at the camp.

Thousands of white settlers came to the Black Hills in search of gold.

Sitting Bull was angry with the settlers for trespassing on Lakota land. His anger grew when the United States wanted to buy the Black Hills. The Lakota refused to sell this land.

The United States ordered all American Indians to reservations. Tired of the fighting, most chiefs and their bands moved to reservations. Sitting Bull and his people did not. The government ordered U.S. soldiers to attack these bands.

Sitting Bull prepared to defend his land. Crazy Horse, a Lakota warrior, supported Sitting Bull's actions.

In 1876, Sitting Bull gathered together other Lakota bands and the Cheyenne for a great war council. The council was held near the Rosebud Creek, located in southern Montana.

CHAPTER 5

Lakota Fight for Their Land

Sitting Bull took part in many Sun Dances. This painting shows a Sun Dance ceremony.

In preparation for the coming war, the Lakota held their wiwanyank wachipi, or Sun Dance ceremony. The Lakota and the Cheyenne gathered together. The Sun Dance ceremony helped the tribes unite and feel strong.

Sitting Bull was among the men who prepared to take part in the Sun Dance. As part of the ceremony, Sitting Bull's friends used their knives to make 50 small cuts between his wrists and shoulders in both of his arms. The cuts on his arms represented Sitting Bull's sacrifice for his tribe.

For that entire day and night, Sitting Bull danced and prayed. During the dance, Sitting Bull drank no water and ate no food. By fasting, he hoped to prove his strength. He wanted Wakantanka to bless his people.

Crazy Horse led a surprise attack against U.S. soldiers in the Battle of the Rosebud.

After dancing for almost two days, Sitting Bull fainted from exhaustion. While unconscious, Sitting Bull had a vision. He saw an army of soldiers falling from the sky with their heads bowed and their hats falling. When Sitting Bull's vision ended and he awoke, Sitting Bull told his people that Wakantanka told him that they would have a victory.

On June 16, 1876, Lakota scouts spotted a group of soldiers. The scouts told Sitting Bull that the soldiers were located near Rosebud Creek in Montana, just 21 miles (34 kilometers) from their camp. Crazy Horse led an attack that surprised the soldiers. Sitting Bull hoped this attack would keep other soldiers away.

Sitting Bull moved his camp toward the Little Bighorn River. At the same time, Lieutenant Colonel Custer was also moving his 600 soldiers toward this river.

The Lakota and Cheyenne conquered Lieutenant Colonel Custer and his troops at the Battle of the Little Bighorn. This painting is one artist's rendition of the Battle of the Little Bighorn.

On June 25, Sitting Bull, the Lakota, and Cheyenne faced more U.S. soldiers. As a chief, Sitting Bull's duty was to protect the women and children. He made sure they were moved away from the battle. He also encouraged his warriors as they rode into battle.

The fighting at the Battle of the Little Bighorn was fierce. Within a matter of hours, Custer and 210 soldiers were dead. The battle continued into the next day. Scouts reported to Sitting Bull that more soldiers were approaching the Lakota camp.

Sitting Bull wanted the fighting to stop. He broke camp. To make sure the soldiers did not follow them, the warriors set fire to the prairie grass.

When moving to new camping grounds, the Northern Plains Indians used horses to pull travois.

The Battle of the Little Bighorn was over. The great American Indian encampment began to break into separate hunting parties. Sitting Bull and his people traveled across Montana, with Colonel Nelson Miles and his regiment of soldiers following closely.

Sitting Bull met with Miles on two occasions. Their first conversation took place on the open prairie. The men talked through the afternoon. Miles tried to convince Sitting Bull to surrender. Sitting Bull refused. He wanted to live freely in the Black Hills and the Powder River country. Sitting Bull was tired of listening to the soldier chief's talk, but he agreed to meet with Miles again the next day.

During their second meeting, Miles warned Sitting Bull that the U.S. government would view his failure to surrender as a hostile act. Miles' threats angered Sitting Bull. He knew the soldier chiefs would not listen. A fight broke out between Miles' soldiers and the Lakota warriors. Following this battle, Sitting Bull led his tribe north in search of safe camping grounds.

CHAPTER 6
Lakota Life Changes

Sitting Bull and one of his wives are pictured outside their tepee at Fort Randall.

Food was scarce for the Lakota during the winter of 1876–1877. Some American Indian bands decided to give in to the white people's demands.

Sitting Bull and his people still refused to go to a reservation. They crossed the border into Canada where they could safely seek shelter. With Sitting Bull and his people out of the country, there were no free American Indians. All were living on reservations. The U.S. government convinced reservation Indian chiefs to sign over the Black Hills and the Powder River country.

Sitting Bull and his people remained in Canada for four years. The reduced size of buffalo herds in Canada made it difficult to find food. Sitting Bull and his people were starving and exhausted.

Sitting Bull watched as small groups of people began to break away from the band to cross the border back to the United States. The returning American Indians were sent to reservations.

On July 19, 1881, Sitting Bull crossed the border to the United States. He had fewer than 200 Lakota people left with him. Sitting Bull and his people traveled to Fort Buford.

They met with Major David Brotherton at Fort Buford. The next day Sitting Bull ordered his son, Crow Foot, to hand his rifle over to the soldiers. This act meant Sitting Bull had surrendered.

During the next two years, Sitting Bull was held at Fort Randall. Life

Sitting Bull surrendered and crossed the border back into the United States. He brought his people to Fort Buford.

there was unpleasant. The Lakota relied on the army to give them food. In 1883, Sitting Bull and his tribe were given permission to join their relatives and friends at Standing Rock Reservation.

In 1885, a man named William F. Cody, nicknamed Buffalo Bill, arrived at the reservation and offered Sitting Bull a job. Buffalo Bill had a Wild West Show that toured the eastern United States and Canada. Sitting Bull saw the

Many American Indians believed the Ghost Dance religion could bring back their old way of life.

show as a chance to escape reservation life.

As a member of the Wild West Show, Sitting Bull earned $50 a week. He gave most of his money to the poor.

Following the tour, Sitting Bull returned to Standing Rock Reservation. He was glad to live a quieter life.

Sitting Bull's happiness soon changed. The U.S. government planned to separate the Great Sioux Reservation into six smaller reservations under the Sioux Act of 1889. Each American Indian family would receive a portion of land. The remaining land would be sold to settlers.

Sitting Bull opposed this action. He spoke out at public meetings. Many Lakota leaders were fearful of the government. The United States bought another 11 million acres (4.5 million hectares) of Lakota land.

Around 1890, a new religion spread through American Indian reservations. White people called this religion the Ghost Dance religion. The Ghost Dance promised that whites would vanish and the buffalo would return.

Wild West Show

In 1885, Sitting Bull joined the Wild West Show. This western theater production featured shooting demonstrations, American Indian dancing, roping, and other events. The show also included reenactments of historic western events, such as the Battle of the Little Bighorn.

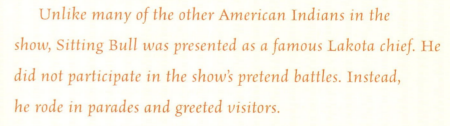

William Cody, better known as Buffalo Bill, began the Wild West Show in 1883. He performed this western theater all over the United States and in Europe. The show lasted for 30 years.

Wild West shows did not portray historic events accurately. The heroes in the Wild West Shows were U.S. soldiers. American Indians played the role of villains.

Unlike many of the other American Indians in the show, Sitting Bull was presented as a famous Lakota chief. He did not participate in the show's pretend battles. Instead, he rode in parades and greeted visitors.

Sitting Bull enjoyed his travels with Buffalo Bill. He became friends with other members of the show, including Annie Oakley. She was best known for her shooting skills.

Sitting Bull enjoyed the public attention he received and the money he earned. He gave much of his money to the poor, and the rest he used to prepare huge feasts for his friends.

Sitting Bull became friends with Buffalo Bill during a tour with the Wild West Show.

Today, Sitting Bull is remembered as a great Lakota leader who fought hard to protect his people and their land.

Government agents knew that Sitting Bull did not start the Ghost Dance religion. But they feared Sitting Bull would take part in an uprising.

On December 15, 1890, Lieutenant Henry Bull Head and 43 Indian police officers came to Sitting Bull's home to arrest him. More than 100 of Sitting Bull's people came to protest.

The men took Sitting Bull outside. Sitting Bull yelled, "I'm not going! Do with me what you like, I'm not going!"

At that moment, a shot hit Lieutenant Bull Head in his side. As Bull Head fell, he turned and shot Sitting Bull. Another police officer shot Sitting Bull in the head. Six police officers and eight of Sitting Bull's people, including his 17-year-old son, Crow Foot, were killed. Sitting Bull, the great Lakota leader, died that morning.

"I wish it to be remembered that I was the last man to surrender my rifle."

—Sitting Bull, 1881

Chronology

1845
Slow counts his first coup. His father performs a name changing ceremony and gives him the name Sitting Bull.

1857
Sitting Bull becomes war chief of the Hunkpapa band.

Late 1860s
Sitting Bull becomes head chief of the Lakota nation.

1872
Sitting Bull proves his bravery during the Battle of Arrow Creek.

1885
Sitting Bull travels with Wild West Show.

1831
Sitting Bull, known as Slow in his childhood, is born in present-day South Dakota.

1852
Sitting Bull becomes a member of the Strong Hearts.

1864
Sitting Bull fights his first battle against U.S. soldiers, who are led by General Sully.

1876
Sitting Bull leads his people in the Battle of the Little Bighorn.

1881
Sitting Bull surrenders. He is sent to Fort Randall.

1890
Sitting Bull dies.

Words to Know

band (BAND)—a group of people, smaller than a tribe

counting coup (KOUNT-ing KU)—an act of bravery when a warrior touches an enemy with his hand or coup stick and escapes unharmed; more than one warrior in a tribe could count coup on the same enemy, and the enemy could be dead or alive.

nomadic (noh-MA-dik)—having a way of life that involves traveling from place to place; the Lakota were a nomadic tribe.

pictograph (PIK-toh-graf)—pictures that tell a story; Sitting Bull drew pictographs to tell about important events in his life.

reservation (rez-ur-VAY-shun)—an area of land set aside for American Indians by the United States government

tepee (TEE-pee)—a cone-shaped tent made of animal skins

trading post (TRAY-ding POHST)—a station set up for exchanging goods

treaty (TREE-tee)—a legal agreement between nations

tribe (TRYB)—a group of people who live in the same area, speak the same language, and obey the same chief

unconscious (uhn-KON-shuhss)—not awake or able to respond to others

To Learn More

Isaacs, Sally Senzell. *America in the Time of Sitting Bull: 1840-1890*. Des Plaines, Ill.: Heinemann Library, 2000.

Marrin, Albert. *Sitting Bull and His World*. New York: Dutton Children's Books, 2000.

Todd, Anne M. *Crazy Horse, 1842-1877*. American Indian Biographies. Mankato, Minn.: Blue Earth Books, 2003.

Todd, Anne M. *Sioux: People of the Great Plains*. American Indian Nations. Mankato, Minn.: Bridgestone Books, 2003.

Internet Sites

Attractions in the West: Sitting Bull
http://www.ndtourism.com/regions/west/WestSittingbull.html

EyeWitness: The Battle of the Little Bighorn, 1876
http://www.ibiscom.com/custer.htm

History of Sitting Bull
http://collections.ic.gc.ca/beaupre/promme92.htm

PBS: New Perspectives on the West
http://www.pbs.org/weta/thewest/people/s_z/sittingbull.htm

Sitting Bull
http://www.powersource.com/gallery/people/sittbull.html

Spectrum Biographies: Sitting Bull
http://www.incwell.com/Biographies/SittingBull.html

Places to Visit

Fort St. Joseph Museum
508 East Main Street
Niles, MI 49120-2618

The Little Bighorn Battlefield National Monument
P.O. Box 39
Exit 510 off I-90 Highway 212
Crow Agency, MT 59022-0039

South Dakota State Historical Society
900 Governors Drive
Pierre, SD 57501-2217

State Historical Society of North Dakota
612 East Boulevard Avenue
Bismarck, ND 58505-0830

Index

Battle of Arrow Creek, 5, 7
Battle of the Little Bighorn, 19, 22–23, 27
Battle of the Rosebud, 21
Bozeman Trail, 18
Bull Head, Henry, 28

Canada, 24–25
Cody, William F., "Buffalo Bill", 25, 27
counting coup, 10, 11
Crazy Horse, 19, 21
Custer, George, 18–19, 21, 22

Dakota Conflict of 1862, 17

Fort Buford, 18, 25
Fort Laramie, 17, 18
Fort Randall, 24, 25

Ghost Dance religion, 26, 28
Great Sioux Reservation, 18, 26

Midnight Strong Heart Society, 13
Miles, Nelson, 23

Northern Pacific Railroad, 4

Oakley, Annie, 27
Oregon Trail, 16

pictograph, 11
Powder River country, 23, 24

Red Cloud, 18
reservation, 18, 19, 24, 25, 26

Sioux Act of 1889, 26
Sitting Bull
    battle, 4–5, 7, 10, 13, 17, 22, 23
    birth, 9
    chief, 4, 13–14, 18
    childhood, 9–10
    death, 28
    family, 9, 10, 11, 12, 14, 25, 28
    holy man, 4, 13
    marriages, 12, 14
    name, 9, 10
South Dakota, 8, 9, 18
    Black Hills, 18–19, 23, 24
Standing Rock Reservation, 25, 26
Strong Hearts, 12, 13
Sully, Alfred, 17
Sun Dance, 20–21

treaties
    Fort Laramie Treaty of 1851, 17
    Fort Laramie Treaty of 1868, 18

vision, 13, 21

Wakantanka, 7, 13, 20, 21
Wild West Show, 25–26, 27